MCO P4400.162

GOVERNMENT-FURNISHED AND -LOANED EQUIPMENT/MATERIEL MANAGEMENT MANUAL (GFE/GFM/LOAN MANUAL)

U.S. MARINE CORPS

PCN 102 052486 00

DEPARTMENT OF THE NAVY
HEADQUARTERS UNITED STATES MARINE CORPS
WASHINGTON, DC 20380-0001

MCO P4400.162B
LPP-2
17 Jul 92

MARINE CORPS ORDER P4400.162B W/CH 1

From: Commandant of the Marine Corps
To: Distribution List

Subj: GOVERNMENT-FURNISHED AND -LOANED EQUIPMENT/MATERIEL
      MANAGEMENT MANUAL (SHORT TITLE: GFE/GFM/LOAN MANUAL)

Ref: (a) SECNAVINST 4440.32
      (b) NavCompt Manual, vol. VIII (NOTAL)
      (c) Federal Acquisition Regulation (FAR)
      (d) DoD Federal Acquisition Regulation Supplement (DFARS)
      (e) DoD 4000.25-2-M
      (f) DoD 5000.12-M
      (g) DoD 4000.25-1-M, ch 11 (AMCL-1)
      (h) MCO 4140.6
      (i) DoD 5105.38-M, ch 12
      (j) MCO 4900.1

Encl: (1) LOCATOR SHEET

Report Required: GFM Status Report (Report Control Symbol
                  DD-4400-37), External Report Control
                  Symbol DD-M (Q1575), par. 1004.4p and apps.
                  D and E

1. <u>Purpose</u>

    a. To publish policies, procedures, responsibilities, and
accounting and reporting instructions in references (a) through
(j) for items being issued or procured in support of Marine
Corps Government-furnished and -loaned equipment/materiel
(GFE/GFM/loan) requirements.

    b. To assign responsibilities for updating policy for
authorizing access to DoD materiel inventories under Defense
contracts, controlling contractor-initiated GFM requisitions,
providing GFM, and informing contract administration offices
(CAO) of materiel shipments to Defense contractors under their
cognizance.

2. <u>Cancellation</u>. MCO P4400.162A and MCO 4400.157B.

3. <u>Applicability</u>. The policies and procedures contained herein
apply to the management/control and accountability of materiel

procured or provided via Military Standard Requisitioning and
Issue Procedures (MILSTRIP) requisitions, purchase orders (PO),
contracts, and military interdepartmental purchase requests
(MIPR). These policies and procedures are in support of Marine
Corps GFE/GFM/loan requirements, contracts, loans, leases, and
bailments of equipment to contractors, Department of Defense
(DoD) military services/agencies, and State and local government
agencies. These policies and procedures also apply to accounting
for GFE/GFM issued within the provisions of other military
services/agencies, contracts and are to be coordinated
by the program managers (PM) and managed by the management
control activity (MCA).

4. <u>Summary of Revision</u>. This revision contains a substantial
number of changes and should be thoroughly reviewed. Changes
include policy on loans, bailment, and leases.

5. <u>Information</u>. These instructions are issued to provide
guidance to personnel in the management of materiel provided as
GFE, GFM, loans, bailments, and leases in behalf of the Marine
Corps.

6. <u>Recommendations</u>. Recommendations concerning the contents
of the Government-Furnished and -Loaned Equipment/Materiel
Management Manual are invited and shall be submitted to the
Commandant of the Marine Corps (CMC) (LPP-2) via the
appropriate chain of command.

7. <u>Reserve Applicability</u>. This Manual is applicable to the
Marine Corps Reserve.

8. <u>Certification</u>. Reviewed and approved this date.

R. J. WINGLASS
Deputy Chief of Staff
for Installations and Logistics

DISTRIBUTION: PCN 10205248600

    Copy to: 7000010 (55)
             7000153 (15)
             8145004, 005 (2)
             7000144/8145001 (1)

R 270240Z FEB 97 ZYB
FM CMC WASHINGTON DC//L//
TO ALMAR
BT
UNCLAS //N04400//
ALMAR 062/97
MSGID/GENADMIN/CMC LPP//
SUBJ/MCO P4400.162 CH 1. GFE-GFM-LOAN MANUAL - INERIM POLICY//
POC/S. BLEVINS/GM13/PRIPHN:DSN 426-1052/PRIFRO:LPP-2/703-696-1052//
RMKS/1. THE PURPOSE OF THIS ALMAR IS TO PROVIDE INTERIM POLICY
INCORPORATING RESPONSIBILITY FOR ALL MARINE CORPS ORGANIZATIONS TO
REPORT DEFENSE CONTRACTOR STATUS CHANGES TO THE MANAGEMENT CONTROL
ACTIVITY (MCA).
2. ADD THE FOLLOWING PAR. TO CURRENT MANUAL:
   PAGE 4-4, PAR. 4001.4 -
ALMAR 062/97
«« --- »»
Date signed: 02/27/97   ALMAR Number: 062/97
CONTRACTOR'S DODAAC."
3. THIS INTERIM POLICY INCORPORATES A RECOMMENDATION FROM THE DODIG
DRAFT REPORT ON MANAGEMENT OF ACCESS TO THE DOD SUPPLY SYSTEM
(PROJECT NO. 3CK-0031.01).//
BT

LOCATOR SHEET

Subj: <u>GOVERNMENT-FURNISHED AND -LOANED EQUIPMENT/MATERIEL
MANAGEMENT MANUAL</u>

Location: _____
(Indicate the location(s) of the copy(ies) of this
Manual.)

ENCLOSURE (1)

GFE/GFM/LOAN MANUAL

RECORD OF CHANGES

Log completed change action as indicated.

Change Number	Date of Change	Date Entered	Signature of Person Incorporated Change

GFE/GFM/LOAN MANUAL

CONTENTS

CHAPTER

APPENDIX

GFE/GFM/LOAN MANUAL

CHAPTER 1

POLICY

CHAPTER 1

POLICY

1000. <u>BACKGROUND</u>

1. Property may be furnished by the Marine Corps only when authorized and when clearly in the best interest of the Marine Corps, the national defense, or the general public, except for foreign military leases which are referred to in chapter 7. Marine Corps property will not be loaned if the loan would not comply with these provisions or if the loaned property would be consumed in use, resulting in unnecessary disposition of property without reimbursement, as could be the case with batteries, petroleum products, and other expendable items. Loans of Marine Corps property are not to be encouraged or promoted.

2. Generally, it is the policy for contractors to furnish all materiel and equipment required for the performance of Government contracts. However, GFE and GFM may be furnished by the Government only when it is determined by cost analysis by the PM/contracting office to be in the best interest of the Government because of economy, standardization, or for expediting production. Special attention will be given to providing materiel and equipment that are determined to be in excess of the approved force acquisition objective stock level (DoD Stores Account Code (SAC) 1 excess list) for contracts that include acquisition, repair, overhaul, modification, or reconditioning.

3. Reclaimed silver will be used as GFM in Marine Corps procurements requiring that metal, per MCO 4555.3.

4. The CMC has designated the Commander, Marine Corps Logistics Bases (COMMARCORLOGBASES) (Code 808-2), Albany, GA, as the MCA for the Marine Corps and the logistics element manager (LEM) for all GFE/GFM requirements. The MCA has been tasked with the responsibility for the administration and accountability of materiel and equipment provided as GFE/GFM/ loan or consigned to contractors or Government repair facilities outside the Marine Corps for purposes of development, manufacture, modernization, modification, repair, overhaul, or bailment.

5. In order for the MCA to maintain control and accountability, all requests for materiel to be consigned to contractors or Government repair facilities outside the Marine Corps for modernization; as peripheral equipment during design, test, acceptance of new equipment, alteration, repair, or overhaul; or loaned to an organization must be forwarded to the MCA (see appendices A and B).

6. The MCA will maintain a central control system over all contractor's access to the DoD supply system (DoD SS). GFE/GFM will not be issued unless authorized by a contract, PO, modification, or amendment and signed by an authorized Government contracting officer. The Marine Corps will perform a loan of materiel to other DoD agencies only when authorized by the MCA and when clearly in the best interest of the Marine Corps. Since GFE/GFM is furnished to a contractor, it should not be confused with a loan. NO MATERIEL OR EQUIPMENT WILL BE LOANED TO A CONTRACTOR. If the Marine Corps is not "contractually obligated" to provide materiel or equipment, it will not be provided.

7. Requests for the loan of principal end items for other services/agencies for which the Marine Corps is the secondary inventory control activity (SICA) should be made directly to the primary inventory control activity (PICA). All attempts should be made to require the PICA to supply their own assets, particularly when the assets are required by the PICA service, even if it is for a joint endeavor.

8. Using-unit-furnished GFE. GFE will not generally be approved if redistribution of assets (borrowing assets from Marine Corps activities) is required. However, in some instances, GFE may be required to be furnished by using units for unique or critical low-density equipment. CMC (LPP) approval is required for using-unit-furnished GFE. Upon notification of the approval, the using unit will transfer accountability of the assets to the MCA. Authorization for transfer and shipping will be provided by the MCA (MCLB (Code 808-2), Albany). The transfer documentation will identify the contract number and identification of the document number directing the transfer.

1001. DEFINITIONS

1. Government-Furnished Equipment. That equipment which fulfills the following requirements:

    a. Government-owned equipment authorized by CONTRACT for use by a commercial/Government contractor.

    b. Title is in or will be taken by the Marine Corps under the terms of the contract.

    c. It is neither consumed during production nor incorporated into any product.

    d. Upon return to the Marine Corps, it will be in the same condition as when delivered to the contractor, subject to normal condition of use in fulfilling the contract.

2. Government-Furnished Materiel. Materiel in the possession of, or acquired by, the Government and later delivered or otherwise

made available to a contractor without reimbursement. GFM is property that may be incorporated into or attached to a deliverable item or that may be consumed or expended in performing a contract. GFM includes assemblies, components, parts, raw and processed materiels, and small tools and assemblies that may be consumed in normal use in performing a contract.

3. <u>Management Control Activity</u>. A Marine Corps activity designated in the contract to validate contractor requisitions to obtain materiel from the DoD SS against contractually specified requirements. The MCA validates DoD-submitted requisitions where the materiel will be shipped to the contractor and initiates requisitions for GFM which would be supplied from the wholesale system. The CMC has designated and charged the MCA with the control, accountability, and administration of the GFE/GFM/loan programs for the Marine Corps per DoD, Department of the Navy (DON), and Marine Corps directives.

4. <u>Loans</u>. The granting of permission to use Marine Corps property without compensation (except for transportation and handling costs) on the condition that it will be returned without cost to the Marine Corps in a condition as good as when loaned--reasonable wear and tear excepted.

5. <u>Temporary Loan</u>. Loans of organic property from one property account to an organization under another command and should not be confused with the loan of wholesale inventory assets. MCO P4400.150 and UM 4400-124 apply.

6. <u>Contributing Contracts</u>. Any contract which supplies materiel to another contract is a contributing contract, and the materiel furnished thereunder is considered GFM.

1002. <u>LOANS</u>

1. Loans will not cause the lender to purchase a replacement item, report table of equipment (T/E) deficiencies, or redistribute assets.

2. Under normal circumstances, the loan of SAC 1 (SAC 1) materiel will not be made to another naval activity. Intra-DON movement of SAC 1 materiel will be either an issue to end use or a transfer to another accountable officer per the NavCompt Manual, volume VIII. Exceptions (i.e., industrial-funded activities) will be handled on a case-by-case basis as provided for in the NavCompt Manual, paragraph 085179.

3. In most cases, SAC 1 assets will not be loaned.

4. Appropriated stores account (ASA) items (SAC 2/3) may be loaned for 1 year and renewed for successive periods not exceeding 1 year at a time.

5. Loan assets will not be shipped until receipt of a fully executed standard Marine Corps loan agreement (appendix C), which will include the following:

    a. Identification of the property loaned, to include national stock number (NSN), nomenclature, quantity, and condition code.

    b. Purpose of the request/loan.

    c. Initial length of loan.

    d. Citation of transportation appropriation.

    e. A statement to the affect that the lender has the right to terminate the loan whenever the property is required.

    f. A point of contact and telephone number.

    g. Borrower's signature or borrower's responsible officer who has acknowledged acceptance of the terms of the loan agreement by signing the agreement.

    h. A statement that the borrower will assume all costs incident to the loan, including the removal of the property from storage or other location, preparation for shipment, transportation, and the return and repair of the property to the condition existing at the time of the loan.

    i. Ship to address: Department of Defense activity address code(s) (DODAAC).

    j. A statement that the borrower will assume all risks of loss or damage and the obligation to replace or reimburse the lender therefor.

1003. <u>EXCLUSIONS</u>

1. This Manual does not apply to temporary issues or loans of materiel for special tooling, special test equipment, and class V materiel, nor should these instructions be utilized in providing software (technical manuals, drawings, etc.) to contractors. This Manual is not applicable to the lease or bailment of facilities or the use of Government production and research property by contractors, nonprofit organizations, foreign governments, or international organizations.

2. <u>Temporary loans</u>. Procedures for control and accountability of temporary loans are provided in MCO P4400.150 and UM 4400-124.

3. DoD policy provides for the issue of materiel in the event of civil (natural disaster) or military emergencies. In either case, normal reimbursement procedures apply. However, in the

case of military emergencies, payment on the part of the
recipient may be deferred per the NavCompt Manual, volume VIII.
Under no circumstances will emergency issues be treated as a loan.

4. Disaster relief participation is an unprogrammed
requirement within the Marine Corps for which no funds are
allocated. These operations will be undertaken on the basis
that the agencies which require military participation will
reimburse the Marine Corps for all costs in addition to the
normal operating expenses.

5. Marine Corps activities are authorized to provide for
emergency issue of stock fund materiel in the event of civil,
military, or natural emergencies. In any case, the issue is
reimbursable even though the actual payment on the part of the
consumer may be deferred. However, in all instances, the
inventory manager is responsible for releasing the property,
maintaining appropriate inventory records (to ensure location
of property), and collecting appropriate reimbursement for
property consumed or for return of the property in a condition
which is unsuitable for return to stock. Guidance for record
management is provided in the NavCompt Manual, volume VIII, and
MCO P4400.159.

1004. <u>TRANSPORTATION</u>. Transportation costs associated with
the shipment of GFE/GFM will be charged to the appropriation
funds contained in the annual Marine Corps bulletin in the 4610
series concerning cargo and personal property transportation
accounting data, assigned to the Marine Corps procurement for
this purpose. Cost for transportation of loaned materiel will
be borne by the borrower.

1005. <u>RESPONSIBILITIES</u>

1. The CMC (LP) will:

   a. Establish policy relating to the issue and control of
GFE/GFM/loan materiel.

   b. Decision all disputes involving the provisions of
GFE/GFM/loans on a case-by-case basis when a request for
support has been denied.

      (1) Within 10 working days of receipt of denial
notice, the requester will provide the MCA with a statement of
the requirement, including its purpose, justification, impact
statement, and a cost analysis.

      (2) The MCA will within 10 working days prepare a
statement of supportability, an impact statement, and
alternatives, if any, and forward both packages to the CMC (LP)
for decisioning.

(3) The CMC (LP) will within 10 working days provide the requester and the MCA a written decision on the dispute and, if approved, the source from which assets will be derived.

c. Provide approval/disapproval for the use of using unit assets for GFE requirements when there are none available from stock.

d. Code LPO will coordinate the submission of the quarterly report for the sale of GFE/GFM and services to U.S. companies to the Defense Security Assistance Agency per current DoD guidance.

2. Marine Corps contracting officers shall:

a. Ensure the provisions of the FAR/DFARS are adhered to and that MCLB (808-2), Albany is identified as the responsible MCA in contractual documents containing GFE/GFM.

b. Include an instructional clause in all contracts where GFE/GFM has been authorized requiring the contractor to do the following:

(1) Acknowledge receipt of GFE/GFM to the MCA.

(2) Report deficiencies in quantity, quality, or failure to the MCA.

(3) Advise the MCA (MCLB (Code 808-2), Albany) when GFE has been shipped from the contractor to a using unit or stock, by forwarding copies of DD Form 1149/DD Form 250 to the MCA.

c. Provide the MCA with a copy of all contracts and modifications thereto where GFE/GFM has been authorized.

d. Stipulate that all contractor-generated requisitions for GFM to supply must be submitted to the MCA rather than to be warehoused or submitted to a source of supply.

e. Identify authorized GFM in the contract or modification by quantity, nomenclature, and NSN where the contractor has authority to requisition GFM through the MCA.

f. Include an instructional clause in all MIPR's/Marine Corps purchase requests (MCPR)/contracts involving GFE/GFM, requiring the contractors to acknowledge receipt of all GFE/GFM materiel by signing and forwarding copies of the DoD Single Line Item Release/Receipt Document (DD Form 1348-1) which accompanies shipments to the MCA GFE/GFM PM.

g. Include "ship to/mark for" instructions for return of GFE/GFM. If return designation is uncertain at the time of issue, the contractor/Defense contract management area office (DCMAO) will be advised to request disposition instructions from the MCA at least 60 days prior to the scheduled termination, or sooner if early return of the materiel is desired. Contracting officers will include the Continuation Sheet (SF 36) with the contract and list the unit cost to the contractor and the GFM unit cost to provide a true cost (price).

h. Provide instructions to mark all containers utilized to return GFE/GFM with the issue document number, procurement instrument identification number (PIIN), and project code.

i. Provide instructions to report any deficiency in quantity, quality, or failure of GFE/GFM to the MCA (MCLB (Code 808-2), Albany, GA 31704).

j. Provide transportation chargeable appropriations data for return of GFE/GFM.

k. Ensure that the MCA reviews/provides data item descriptions (DID) for all contractual documentation prior to request for proposal (RFP)/request for bid (RFB) and/or establishment of any binding agreement.

1. Notify the CMC (LPO) if, in the course of the contract, GFE/GFM becomes the subject to direct commercial sale to a foreign customer.

3. The Commander, Marine Corps Systems Command (COMMARCORSYSCOM) and Direct Reporting Program Manager Advance Amphibious Assault (DRPM AAA) PM's shall:

a. Ensure that, during the program objective memorandum cycle, funds are programmed to satisfy valid requirements for all GFE/GFM, including those items to be procured by MCLB, Albany.

b. Determine the requirements for all GFE/GFM/ loan materiel for support of acquisition/modification projects. Requirements for GFE/GFM will be determined in the same fiscal year that requirements are developed for the parent end item (i.e., preparation of letter of adoption and procurement and integrated logistics support plan) and will be maintained current throughout the acquisition process to ensure adequate funding is provided.

c. Submit reservation requests for GFE/GFM per paragraph 2000, following, to the MCA (MCLB (Code 808-2) Albany) (see appendix A).

d. Provide the MCA copies of MIPR's, requests for contractual procurement (RCP), acceptances, contracts, and amendments/modifications that apply to GFE/GFM.

e. Submit reservation/request for shipment of loan materiel per paragraph 2000, following, to the MCA (see appendix B).

    f.   Include the following on the procurement instructions:

    (1) Information that establishes the Marine Corps procuring or contracting officer as the point of contact for GFE/GFM. All GFE/GFM/loan requests will be submitted to the MCA. An information copy will be provided to the contracting officer. All contracts are required to:

    (a) Identify the MCA (MCLB (Code 808-2) (RIC MPM)).

    (b) Stipulate that all contractor-generated requisitions for GFM to the supply system must be submitted to the MCA rather than to be warehoused or submitted to a source of supply.

    (c) Identify authorized GFM in the contract or modification by quantity, nomenclature, and NSN where the contractor has authority to requisition GFM through the MCA.

    (d) Advise the MCA (MCLB (Code 808-2), Albany) when GFE has been shipped from the contractor to a using unit or stock by forwarding copies of DD Form 1149/DD Form 250 to the MCA.

    (2) An instructional clause in all MIPR's/MCPR's/contracts involving GFE/GFM, requiring the contractors to acknowledge receipt of all GFE/GFM materiel by signing and forwarding copies of the DoD Single Line Item Release/Receipt Document (DD Form 1348-1) which accompanies shipments to the MCA GFE/GFM PM.

    (3) "Ship to/mark for" instructions for return of GFE/GFM. If return designation is uncertain at the time of issue, the contractor/DCMAO will be advised to request disposition instructions from the MCA at least 60 days prior to the scheduled termination, or sooner if early return of the materiel is desired. Contracting officers will include the Continuation Sheet (SF 36) with the contract, listing the unit cost to the contractor and the GFM unit cost to provide a true cost (price).

    (4) Instructions to mark all containers utilized to return GFE/GFM with issue document number, PIIN, and project code.

    (5) Instructions to report any deficiency in quantity, quality, or failure of GFE/GFM to the MCA (MCLB (Code 808-2), Albany).

    (6) Transportation chargeable appropriations data for return of GFE/GFM.

    g.   Provide funding at least 30 days prior to the required delivery date (RDD), by allotment, to the MCA when acquisition of SAC 1 or 2 items is required to satisfy GFE/GFM requirements.

   h. Submit requests for shipment of GFE/GFM per paragraph 2000, following, to the MCA for Headquarters Marine Corps (HQMC) contracts or other service/Marine Corps joint contracts.

4. The COMMARCORLOGBASES, Albany serves as the MCA PM and shall:

   a. Perform the LEM functions for the Marine Corps GFE/GFM/loan programs.

   b. Take appropriate action to acquire, position, ship, and account for all SAC 1 and 2 items. Take appropriate action to receive, reserve, and account for all SAC 3 items and ship when requested by the contracting officer.

   c. Administer the GFE/GFM/loan materiel program within the Marine Corps per the NavCompt Manual, volume VIII, FAR, DFARS, and this Manual. In addition, item accountability will be maintained on the accountable inventory record by appropriate purpose/condition codes for GFE/GFM/loan materiel through final disposition. Ensure stores accounting financial inventory records are reconciled semiannually with the inventory record balances and the dollar value of materiel adjusted on hand. Inventory records control of GFE/GFM/loan materiel ensures positive financial accountability.

   d. Assign Marine Corps project codes to all requests for reservation/shipment of GFE/GFM/loan materiel per DoD 4000.25-2-M and DoD 5000.12-M.

   e. Load requirements for GFE/GFM/loan materiel to the project requirements file (PRF) when supply action is not required within 90 days.

   f. Notify the requester of the project code assigned each reservation/shipment of GFE/GFM/loan materiel.

   g. Advise the requester of the attainment of materiel to satisfy reservations requested for GFE/GFM/loan materiel.

   h. Notify the requester immediately when materiel cannot be obtained or shipped in time to meet the RDD assigned to GFE/GFM/loan requirements.

   i. Coordinate the return of GFE/GFM residue/loan materiel.

   j. Investigate discrepancy reports related to GFE/GFM/loan materiel submitted by the contractor/DCMAO and forward the results of the investigation to the appropriate contracting agency with recommended corrective action within 10 days of discrepancy notification.

k. Initiate follow-up action when confirmation of receipt of GFE/GFM/loan materiel has not been reported by the consignee within 30 days after the expected time of arrival.

l. Maintain fiscal and supply accountability for all GFE/GFM/loan materiel. Billing and payment procedures will be per the NavCompt Manual, volume VIII, MCO P4400.72, MCO P4400.159, and as covered by contractual agreements.

m. Provide disposition instructions for the return of GFE/GFM/loan materiel when such instructions are not provided by contract or when changes to these become necessary. Instructions will include a requirement for the shipper to mark containers/equipment with the PIIN, Marine Corps project code, and issuing document number.

n. Provide cost data to the requester for all SAC 1 and 2 GFE/GFM requirements.

o. Provide to the CMC (LCS), by 1 December each calendar year, a consolidated listing of all GFE/GFM projects by commodity area. The listing will identify all SAC 1 and 2 items by project, to include a current unit price and total price for each item as described in chapter 4, following, and appendices D and E. Report Control Symbol DD-4400-37 has been assigned to this report.

p. Maintain a central control system over all contractors' access to the DoD SS.

q. Deny any GFM issues that would exceed the quantity limitation provided in the contractual agreement.

r. Approve and direct all requests and extensions for shipment/reservation of loaned materiel.

s. Execute loan agreements with borrowers/consignees per the NavCompt Manual, paragraph 085179.

t. Identify authorized GFM in the contract or modification by quantity, nomenclature, and NSN where the contractor has authority to requisition GFM through the MCA.

u. Validate all requisitions for GFM to be provided to contractors to ensure they are contractually authorized.

v. Provide instructions to mark all containers utilized to return GFE/GFM with issue document number, PIIN, and project code.

w. Review/provide DID requirements for all Marine Corps contractual documents (i.e., contracts, statements of work, etc.) prior to RFP/RFB and/or establishment of any binding agreements involving GFE/GFM.

CHAPTER 2

GFE/GFM/LOAN REQUEST PROCEDURES

CHAPTER 2

GFE/GFM/LOAN REQUEST PROCEDURES

2000. INFORMATION

1. Contracts requiring GFE/GFM may originate at HQMC, MARCORSYSCOM, DRPM AAA, MARCORLOGBASES, Albany, or as a contract from another service/Defense Logistics Agency procuring/contracting centers/agencies/or other commands for and on behalf of the Marine Corps. Loan requests may originate at MARCORSYSCOM or other agencies, but no loan assets will be issued until a signed loan agreement is received by the MCA (appendix C). Acquisition of materiel will be done only when it is the most effective manner to accomplish the task. When SAC 1 materiel will be incorporated into another end item or when the item will not be recovered, appropriate identification of this fact will be made on the reservation/request for shipment. The funding provided is the same as that which finances the procurement of the end item. Such funding will be utilized to reimburse the stock fund expenditure at the time the materiel is released from the stock fund or when materiel is requisitioned from the source of supply.

2. All requests for reservation/shipment of GFE/GFM are to be submitted to the MCA utilizing appendix A or B, as appropriate.

3. Loan requests are received from other services within DoD and authorized Government agencies in instances where it is in the best interest of the Government to satisfy special test, projects, and production requirements necessitating Marine Corps assets. These instances occur when it is more economical to use existing assets for short periods of time, rather than procuring and disposing of additional assets.

4. All requests for the requirements listed in paragraph 2000.2, preceding, are to be submitted to the MCA. Materiel with an RDD of 90 days or more will be identified, and a request for reservation will be prepared and information provided in the format shown in appendix A. Materiel with an RDD of less than 90 days will be identified, a request for direct shipment will be prepared, and information will be provided in the format shown in appendix B.

2001. DETERMINATION OF ASSET AVAILABILITY

1. Upon receipt of an authorized reservation/shipment request, a determination of asset availability will be made by the MCLB, Albany inventory manager, to include screening DoD inventories for GFM assets to achieve more cost-effective systems and equipment acquisitions. These assets will be utilized in lieu of procurement in acquisition programs for military-designed

and commercial materiel. The determination that Marine Corps assets are available for loan does not, in itself, justify providing the materiel. Consideration for approval by the MCA includes:

    a. Adverse effects on readiness posture.

    b. Adequate asset positions.

    c. Availability of funds for reimbursement for transportation, loss, repair, or reconditioning by the requester.

    d. Prescribed timeframe for the loan period.

    e. Exhaustion of all other support sources by the borrower.

    f. Readily replacing stocks when war reserve assets are required.

    (1) Requests that will require the use of war reserve assets will be primarily for GFE requirements only.

    (2) Normally, loans of war reserve assets will not be authorized.

    g. Proof that the furnishing of all materiel (particularly GFM) is in the best interest of the Government because of economy, standardization, or expediting production.

    h. Special attention given to materiel in excess or the approved force acquisition objective.

2. When Marine Corps assets are not available for GFE, materiel will not normally be procured or redistributed from using units to satisfy the requirement; and the GFE request will be denied. The CMC (LPP) must be contacted for permission to redistribute assets from a using unit for GFE requirements. When this is required, the using unit will transfer accountability of the assets to the MCA once approval is received from the CMC (LPP). Authorization for transfer and shipping will be provided by the MCA (MCLB (Code 808-2), Albany). The transfer documentation will identify the contract number and identification of the document directing the transfer. When Marine Corps assets are not available for GFE requirements, the MCA will notify the requester and, in coordination with the contracting officer requisition the required item from an integrated materiel manager. In such instances, the contractor will be authorized to provide all materiel. Circumstances may dictate authorizing a contractor to utilize the DoD SS per chapter 4.

3. Upon approval of the request, action will be taken to effect an immediate issue of GFE/GFM/loan materiel or reserve materiel in the system for future use. If assets are available from Purpose

Code K (reserve for loan), the release of the materiel will establish a "due."

4. Applicable GFE/GFM/loan requirements will be loaded to the PRF by the MCLB, Albany inventory manager when supply action is not required within 90 days. The data loaded to the PRF must include the RDD, quantity, fund code/cost analysis code (CAC), media and status code, management transaction code, hot/cold indicator, priority, project code, and PM code.

CHAPTER 3

MARINE CORPS LOGISTICS BASE, ALBANY, MANAGEMENT PROCEDURES

CHAPTER 3

MARINE CORPS LOGISTICS BASE, ALBANY, MANAGEMENT PROCEDURES

3000. ESTABLISHING DUES TO THE STORES SYSTEM

1. The MCA will ensure due-in records are established on the inventory record. The dues will identify:

   a. GFE being returned after completion of contracts.

   b. Residue (unused) GFM being returned after completion of contracts.

   c. Materiel on loan.

   d. Materiel due based on initiated procurement instruments. Further, the MCA will ensure that due transactions contain the appropriate management codes to identify due-ins that involve GFE/GFM.

   e. Assembly/disassembly.

   f. Conversion.

   g. Modification.

   h. Repair.

   i. Test.

2. The MCLB, Albany establishes these dues as a result of:

   a. Documentation authorizing GFE/GFM/loans.

   b. Copies of contracts.

   c. Particular shipment disposition instructions furnished a contractor or borrower.

   d. Assembly/disassembly.

   e. Conversion.

   f. Modification.

   g. Repair.

   h. Test.

3. The MCA will utilize copies of all applicable contracts and related correspondence (i.e., contract modifications, cancellations, etc.) to ensure timely updates to the dues record.

3001. IMMEDIATE ISSUES OF GFE/GFM/LOANS

1. When GFE/GFM/loan requirements have an RDD which precludes establishment of a PRF reservation, the MCA will take immediate supply action. If materiel is available, the MCA will release the GFE/GFM. Loan assets will be shipped only after a signed loan agreement (appendix C) is received.

2. Supply transactions will be assigned new document numbers by the inventory manager. Original contract or MIPR document numbers cannot be perpetuated in Data Columns (DC) 30-44 of supply transactions.

3. The remarks block of all GFE/GFM/loan issues must cite the appropriate transaction, appropriation data, as well as the consignee and, for GFE/GFM, the applicable contract number and MIPR or RCP number, when applicable. DC's 45-50 (supplementary address) will contain the contractor's identity code or loan consignee's activity address code (AAC). In order to comply with this requirement, off-line materiel release orders (MRO) may be used to ensure timely and accurate processing by all activities. The types of transactions utilized in making issues are contained in paragraph 3004.2a, following.

4. Supply transactions will cite the assigned project code and management transaction codes as follows:

SAC (End Item)	Management Transaction Code
1	K
2	L
3	J

5. Supply transactions will contain a signal code and cost analysis/fund code per the following criteria. A CAC provides an accessible means of classifying losses/gains for supply management analysis. These codes are assigned to nonreimbursable transactions on MRO's or supply transactions. Appendix E of UM 4400-71 contains a listing of available codes.

Item Issued	End Item	Signal Code	Fund Code
ASA 1/	SFA 2/	M	Appropriate CAC.
ASA	ASA	M	Appropriate CAC.
SFA	SFA	M	Appropriate CAC.
SFA	ASA	L	Issues citing Signal Code L require the fund code financing the procurement of the end item.

1/ Appropriated store account.

2/ Stock fund account.

6. MCA GFE/GFM/loans for testing purposes will cite in the issue transactions the appropriate CAC.

7. The MCA initiates the requirements release transaction to meet established RDD's.

3002. RETURN RECEIPTS OF GFE/GFM/LOANS

1. General Information

    a. GFE/GFM/loan materiel will be returned to the distribution system in several categories:

        (1) End items being returned after completion of contracts, incorporating GFM previously furnished to the contractor.

        (2) System residue (unused) GFM being returned after completion of contracts.

        (3) Loans being returned.

        (4) Loan assets selected to satisfy priority demand from the Fleet Marine Force.

        (5) System GFE upon completion of requirements.

    b. For each of these categories, a due will have been established.

    c. Thirty days prior to the expiration of the loan period, or if notified by the borrower of a pending loan return, the MCA PM will contact the borrower and provide shipping instructions for return of the loaned materiel. These instructions will also request that advance copies of the shipping document(s) be furnished to the PM.

d. If in the course of the contract GFE/GFM becomes subject to direct commercial sale to a foreign customer, the CMC (LPO) should be notified. DoD 7290.3-M applies.

2. Processing the Materiel Request Confirmation (MRC). As a result of processing the MRC to the document control file (DCF), master inventory file, and the master stores file, the MCA GFE/GFM/loan PM will ensure status transactions are produced for further processing within MCLB, Albany.

3003.   STATUS TO THE MCA (MCLB, ALBANY) GFE/GFM/LOAN PROGRAM MANAGER

1. Concept. The MCA GFE/GFM/loan coordinator must be aware of Marine Corps materiel in the hands of contractors/other Government facilities and borrowers. To facilitate this, a record will be maintained within MCLB, Albany. Issues and receipts of GFE/GFM/loans through the Subsystem 03/04 process will produce status transactions for delivery within MCLB, Albany, to the Office of the Executive Director for Financial Management (Code 448). Once the information from this status has been recorded, the Office of the Executive Director for Financial Management (Code 448) will forward pertinent status to the PM (Code 808-2).

2. Issues. The Subsystem 03/04 process resulting from an issue of GFE/GFM/loans will produce PM status transactions, identified as follows:

GFM: Document Identifier Code (DIC) Z6Z (reimbursable items) (SAC 1)

GFE/GFM: DIC Z8Z (nonreimbursable items) (SAC's 1, 2, and 3)

Loans: DIC Z8Z (nonreimbursable items) (SAC's 1, 2, and 3)

3. Receipts. The Subsystem 03/04 process, resulting from receipt of GFE/GFM/loans, will produce the following PM status

a. DIC Z9Z (Results From Processing DIC D4S MRC's). Delivery of end item from prime contractor upon completion of required work.

b. DIC Z9Z (Results From Processing DIC D6H MRC's). Return of residue (unused) GFM from test/repair and return from loan.

4. Other Notices of Shipment/Receipt. When contracts require one contractor to furnish materiel to another contractor, the delivery of GFE/GFM from one contractor to another will also be reported to the MCA. A DD Form 250 (Materiel Inspection and

Receiving Report) will be mailed to the MCA, MCLB, Albany. While the materiel is not being physically picked up by the Marine Corps Distribution System, it is imperative that stores records reflect the delivery to the new contractor. To facilitate this stores requirement, the MCA will, upon receipt of DD Form 250, identify and annotate the applicable project code; post data to the record; and forward the DD Form 250 to the Executive Director for Financial Management (Code 448), MCLB, Albany, where the two transactions (a receipt confirmation (DIC B4S) to MPB and an issue transaction to (DIC B7_)) will be processed to cause the movement of money value to account M99. These transactions, to be processed simultaneously, will be logged in the MCLB, Albany, stores records and will produce the necessary DIC Z6Z/Z8Z PM status transactions.

5. Status Transactions. These transactions are for control and accountability.

3004. STORES ACCOUNTING FUNCTIONS

1. General Information

    a. As stated in MCO P4400.159, chapter 6, special MCLB, Albany stores accounting procedures are necessary to keep a record stores system materiel suspended in work where item control is not maintained on the MCLB, Albany inventory control records. Materiel issued from stocks as either GFE/GFM/loans will be carried in stores as a transfer of location to account M99. The exception to this rule concerns those transactions that involve GFM item(s) issued to assembly/disassembly/ conversion/modification, within the Marine Corps, which will be carried in stores as a transfer of location to account M98. The accounts M98 and M99 are money value only (MVO) accounts. The purpose of these accounts is to track assets out of the stores systems. Account M94 is utilized to record emergency issues of prepositioned war reserve, and account M97 is used for emergency mobilization issues. Refer to MCO P4400.159 for more detailed information.

    b. The CAC provides the "key" to maintaining accurate M98 and M99 accounts. The CAC for the M99 account is assigned by the MCA. The MCLB, Albany comptroller is notified of actions affecting account M99 upon receipt of the receipt transactions (DIC's Z6Z, Z8Z, Z9Z, and Z4S) or the DD Form 250 on contributing contracts from the PM. The status transactions are byproducts of the Subsystem 03/04 automated processing of issues from or receipts to the MCLB, Albany inventory and stores accounting files.

2. <u>Issues</u>

a. Issue transactions processed against the wholesale inventory records of the MCLB, Albany subsystem under the following DIC's increase the dollar accountability in account M99:

<u>DIC</u>	<u>Description of Transaction</u>
D7G	Issues for destructive test/evaluation.
D7H	Issues of GFE/GFM repair parts.
D7L	Issues for assembly/disassembly/ conversion/modification.
D7M	Issues to repair/test.
D7N	Issues to loan.

b. As the transactions progress through the MCLB, Albany stores accounting process, the value of the materiel is dropped or transferred to the appropriate purpose or condition code in the Marine Corps Distribution System; and a simultaneous increase adjustment) transaction for the same value is recorded in account M99. A byproduct of this process is a status transaction (DIC Z6Z/Z8Z) which is forwarded to the MCA PM, then on to the Executive Director for Financial Management (Code 481), Albany. This status transaction identifies the NSN, project code, quantity transferred, and the document number under which the materiel moved. The comptroller will maintain these status transactions in a manual file.

3. <u>Receipts</u>

a. Receipt transactions processed against the wholesale inventory records of the Inventory Control Subsystem, under the following DIC's, increase the item accountability in the Inventory Control Subsystem and decrease the dollar accountability in the M99 account within the Stores Accounting Subsystem:

<u>DIC</u>	<u>Description of Transaction</u>
D4M	Return from test/repair (end item).
D6G	Return from destructive test/evaluation.
D6H	Return residue, unused GFM.
D6L	Return from assembly/disassembly.

DIC	Description of Transaction
D6M	Return from repair/test.
D6N	Return from loan.

b. When a receipt transaction citing DIC D4M, D6H, D6M, or D6N is recorded in stores, the value of the GFE/Government-loaned materiel will be reduced automatically from the M99 account by the generating DIC D9Z (adjustment loss) transaction.

c. When a receipt transaction citing DIC D6L is recorded in stores, the value of the return from assembly/disassembly/conversion/modification materiel is processed to the Stores Accounting Subsystem, increasing the distribution stocks available for issue. The stores accounting process will produce a DIC Z6L PM status transaction (format will be the same as that used for DIC Z9Z), which will be forwarded to the MCA.

d. The M99 Account Program Manager (Code 808-2), MCLB, Albany will match the holding (suspense) file applicable to the project code and remove the DIC Z8Z transactions. The Executive Director for Financial Management (Code 448), MCLB, Albany will upon receipt of the transactions effect necessary accounting procedures as referenced in MCO P4400.159.

CHAPTER 4

CONTROL OF ACCESS TO DOD MATERIEL INVENTORIES
REQUIRED BY DEFENSE CONTRACTS

CHAPTER 4

CONTROL OF ACCESS TO DOD MATERIEL INVENTORIES
REQUIRED BY DEFENSE CONTRACTS

4000. PURPOSE. To update policy, procedures, and responsibilities for controlling and monitoring GFM issued from supply systems inventories and informing CAO's of materiel shipments to Defense contractors under their cognizance.

1. No GFM is provided to contractors unless such action is clearly in the best interest of the Marine Corps.

2. Contractors are not allowed direct access to the DoD SS for GFM.

3. GFM to be provided to contractors is identified by nomenclature, NSN, and quantity or specified level in the contract or modification.

4. All requisitions for GFM to be provided to contractors are validated to ensure they are contractually authorized.

5. All GFM requisitions into the DoD SS originated by a contractor or to be shipped to a contractor will be validated. SECNAVINST 4440.32 and DoD 5000.12-M apply.

4001. RESPONSIBILITIES

1. The MARCORSYSCOM and DRPM AAA shall:

   a. Determine if providing GFM (in excess of the approved force acquisition objective stock level) is in the best interest of the Government and thoroughly document the rationale and justification for this decision.

   b. Provide the contracting officer a detailed list of authorized GFM for inclusion in solicitations per subpart 45.303-2 of the FAR. The list must identify GFM by NSN, nomenclature, and quantity or specified level.

   c. Request that all contracts requiring GFE/GFM identify the MCA, MCLB, Albany, GA 31704.

2. The MCA shall:

   a. Maintain files that document the quantity of materiel issued to contractors. The files will contain contract number, requisition number, unit prices, and all pertinent shipping and receipt information.

b. Ensure that requisitions which furnish GFM to contractors from the supply system are screened to verify that they are within the contractually authorized levels of each contract.

c. Pass or refer validated requisitions to the appropriate source for supply action. Requisitions which fail validation shall be rejected.

d. Respond to MILSTRIP source of supply validation inquiries, following DoD 4000.25-1-M, chapter 11.

e. Provide reports to CAO's following the guidance contained in appendices D and E. The reports shall be prepared for the periods ending 31 March, 30 June, 30 September, and 31 December.

f. Validate requisitions and shipments for materiel from the DoD SS that submitted by a contractor or to be shipped to a contractor against contractually specified requirements.

g. Provide contracting officers with the contractor's DODAAC for contracts that authorize GFM.

h. Generate MILSTRIP GFM referral validation inquiries (DIC AX1) to the appropriate source of supply.

3. Contracting officers shall:

a. Ensure that the MCA is identified in contracts that authorize GFM. Stipulate in the contract any permitted delegation of the MCA responsibility. Include the MCA on distribution for all modifications related to GFM.

b. Ensure that a list of identifiable GFM (by document number, nomenclature, and quantity) and applicable requisitioning procedures are included in the contract.

c. Require in the contract that requisitions for GFM from the supply system submitted by a contractor, or shipped to a contractor, must be submitted to the MCA.

d. Request the MCA provide the contractor's DODAAC to the contracting officer.

4. All other Marine Corps organizations (to include inventory managers): shall submit Defense contractor status change to the Marine Corps MCA within 10 days after contract award, completion, change, or termination. Status canges should include the Defense contractor's DODAAC.

CHAPTER 5

PROPERTY LOANED TO VETERANS ORGANIZATIONS

CHAPTER 5

PROPERTY LOANED TO VETERANS ORGANIZATIONS

5000. <u>BACKGROUND</u>

1. <u>Authority</u>. Government property may be loaned to recognized national veterans organizations for use at national or State conventions or national youth athletic or recreation tournaments, as prescribed i paragraphs 5000.2 through 5002, following. Loans are not authorized for other types of conventions (see appendix F).

2. <u>Recognized Organizations</u>. The provisions of these regulations apply to the veterans organizations identified in appendix F and their youth affiliates with permission of the parent organizations.

3. <u>Items To Be Loaned</u>. The following items, suitable substitutes, or similar items are authorized to be loaned, if available:

    a. Cots.

    b. Mattresses.

    c. Mattress covers.

    d. Blankets.

    e. Pillows.

    f. Folding chairs.

    g. Tentage.

5001. <u>PROCEDURES</u>

1. <u>Requests for Loan of Property</u>. Requests by authorized organizations for the loan of Marine Corps property will be submitted to COMMARCORLOGBASES (Code 808-2/MCA), Albany, GA 31704 via a local Marine Corps activity adjacent to the area in which the convention is to be held. When practicable, requests will be submitted at least 90 days prior to the date the loan is desired. Such requests will contain the following information:

    a. Name of the organization making the application.

    b. Location at which the convention will be held.

    c. Period during which the loan will be required.

    d. Number of individuals to be accommodated.

e.   Type and quantity of each item desired.

f.   Type of convention (national or State).

g.   Explicit instructions pertaining to the point of delivery to the representative of the requesting organization.

h.   Any other pertinent information considered necessary to assure prompt delivery of the required property.

2.   Determination of Availability

a.   Commander's Actions. Upon receipt of a request for loan of property, the commander of the Marine Corps activity receiving the request will initiate action to determine the availability of all property requested. If property is available at the local command level, the local commander may complete the loan process/procedure. When property is not available at the local level or assistance is required, the local Marine Corps commander will submit to the MCA (MCLB, Albany) a request for reservation/shipment of all items for which approval of the loan is recommended. The MCA, upon receipt of such requests, will determine the availability of the items and will designate the appropriate source of supply for the quantities of items authorized to be loaned.

b.   Determination of Nonavailability. In no case will a determination of nonavailability be made, unless fully justified.

c.   Tentage. When tentage is required, approval of the loan and of the types of tentage to be made available will be made by the MCA.

3.   Processing of Loans

a.   Notification. When the commander of the Marine Corps activity has received information on the availability of property requested for loan, the requesting organization will be notified of the following:

(1) That the loan of the property must involve no expense to the Marine Corps.

(2) The items and quantities available for loan and the source from which supply of the property will be effected.

(3) The estimated costs which will be required to be paid by the requesting organization to cover transportation of the property from the source of supply to destination and return.

(4) That the requesting organization must furnish sufficient guards and such other personnel as may be necessary to protect, maintain, and operate the property involved in the loan.

(5) That the requesting organization must pay all charges for water, gas, heat, and electric current (if furnished), based on meter readings or such other methods as may be determined.

(6) That the period of the loan is limited to 15 days from date of delivery to the organization, except under unusual circumstances.

(7) That used property will be loaned in all cases, when available.

(8) That, upon termination of their use, the requesting organization will be required to vacate the premises loaned, to remove all of its own property therefrom, and to turn over all Marine Corps property.

(9) That cost of renovation and repair, after use by the convention, will be at the expense of the using organization and that renovation and repair must be accomplished in a manner specified by the MCA and/or the commander of the Marine Corps activity handling the request so as to expedite the return of the items.

(10) That any transportation costs in connection with the repair and renovation of the property will also be at the expense of the using organization.

b. Execution of Agreement. When the requesting organization has been made aware of the conditions under which the loan will be effected, an agreement embodying the foregoing conditions will be executed by the MCA and/or the local commander of the Marine Corps activity and an authorized representative of the requesting organization.

5002. RESPONSIBILITIES

1. Responsibilities of the Supply Officer. The supply officer of the Marine Corps activity authorized to make loans of Marine Corps property to requesting organizations, as prescribed in paragraphs 5002.1a through d, following, will maintain an account of all property furnished to requesting organizations. The supply officer will use the invoice and receipt forms prepared to transfer property to the custody of the requesting organization as a basis for accountability. The supply officer will be responsible for obtaining from the requesting organization the necessary copies of the receipt forms based upon a joint inventory. The supply officer is further responsible for the following:

a. Liaison. Maintaining liaison with the requesting organization during the period of utilization of the loaned Marine Corps Property.

b. _Inventory_. Preparing, in cooperation with a representative of a requesting organization, a joint inventory of property being returned. Such joint inventory will serve as the basis for a final receipt at the expiration of the loan. All copies will be certified as to correctness, both by the supply officer and the organization representative with whom the inventory is taken.

c. _Return_. Ensuring that, at the close of the convention, all returned property is shipped, at the expense of the requesting organization, to the source of supply directly or through repair facilities. (Shipping documents covering such shipments will be prepared by the property officer and will clearly indicate the project code and the convention from which return has been effected.)

d. _Cost_. Determining the cost of and making formal demand upon the requesting organization for the following:

(1) Items lost, destroyed, or damaged beyond prospect of economical repair.

(2) Costs, for all items, of the renovation or repair accomplishment at Government repair facilities. Estimated costs will be obtained from such facilities as soon as practicable for the purpose of making demand for payment.

2. _Collections_. Collections made by the supply officer will be reported to and the proceeds deposited with the local disbursing officer. If payment is not received within a reasonable time, the matter will be referred to the next higher command for appropriate action. All collections under these provisions for loan of Marine Corps property will be credited to the applicable Marine Corps general fund receipt account.

CHAPTER 6

REPLENISHMENT PARTS PURCHASE OR BORROW (RPPOB) PROGRAM
(BAILMENT PROGRAM)

CHAPTER 6

REPLENISHMENT PARTS PURCHASE OR BORROW (RPPOB) PROGRAM
(BAILMENT PROGRAM)

6000. BACKGROUND. Section 1216(a) of Public Law 98-525, Defense Procurement Reform Act of 1984 of 19 October 1984, as codified in title 10 U.S.C. 2320(d), states: "The Secretary of Defense shall establish programs which provide domestic business concerns an opportunity to purchase or borrow replenishment parts from the United States for the purpose of design replication or modification, to be used by such concerns in the submission of States..." The RPPOB Program (bailment) was established to implement the requirements of this public law.

6001. POLICY

1. Only domestic businesses may participate in the RPPOB Program.

2. Through the RPPOB Program, the Marine Corps shall make sample parts available to domestic businesses for the purpose of design replication, modification, or development and submission of a data package to obtain approval to sell like replenishment parts to the Government.

3. To provide the maximum incentive for industry to participate in the RPPOB Program, the Marine Corps shall assure all qualified companies are provided the opportunity to complete for parts they have made competitive under the RPPOB Program. Accordingly, no part shall be procured under requirements so strict as to eliminate the firm that moved the part from noncompetitive to competitive status through a successful RPPOB action.

4. The Marine Corps must be the PICA of the part to approve requests from potential suppliers to view or obtain sample parts on a bailment or purchase basis.

6002. INFORMATION

1. The policy and procedures on the RPPOB Program are contained in MCO 4140.6

    a. MCO 4140.6 states that the COMMARCORLOGBASES (Code 812), Albany will operate this program.

    b. Potential supplies must submit, in writing, a request to buy or borrow an item to the COMMARCORLOGBASES (Code 812), Albany, GA 31704.

    c. The potential supplier is required to sign the bailment/ sales agreement and submit a certified check (payable to the "Treasurer of the United States" in the amount determined by Code 812) to the COMMARCORLOGBASES (Code 812), Albany, GA 31704.

2. A potential supplier may not borrow items under warranty. The Government will not sell items under warranty unless the same item not under warranty is not available. In those instances where a warranted item is sold, the warranty does not transfer with the sale. A warranted item will not be precluded from being viewed.

6-4

CHAPTER 7

LEASES

CHAPTER 7

LEASES

7000. FOREIGN MILITARY LEASES

1. MCO 4900.1 and DoD 5105.38-M provide policy, procedures, and guidance for the loan of Marine Corps assets to foreign countries. For clarification purposes, the following information is provided:

    a. Use of leases. Normally, the U.S. Government makes Defense articles available to foreign governments by foreign military sales under the Arms Export Control Act (AECA). However, there may be exceptional instances in which a lease agreement would be the most appropriate method whereby U.S. Defense articles can be made available to foreign countries or international organizations. Such arrangements are authorized under the AECA, chapter 6, when it is determined that there are compelling foreign policy and national security reasons for providing such articles on a lease rather than a sales basis, and the articles are not needed at this time for public use. For example, a foreign government may desire to obtain a Defense article for a short period under a lease for testing purposes to assist it in determining whether to procure the article in quantity. As another example, the U.S. Government may only be able to respond to an urgent foreign requirement for Defense property by making it available from inventory but for national defense reasons cannot sell the property and must require its return to inventory after a specified term. Leases of Defense articles to foreign countries or international organizations will be concluded under the AECA, chapter 6; leases (or loans) to foreign countries or international organizations under 10 U.S.C. 2667 are not authorized.

    b. The country or international organization must pay in U.S. dollars all costs incurred by the U. S. Government in leasing such articles, including reimbursement for depreciation of such articles while leased (the rental payment). The charge for depreciation will be based on the current procurement value, actual acquisition cost (if known), or latest procurement cost. If there is a current procurement contract in effect for the DoD component for an item which is identical to the property to be leased, the current procurement price will be applied, adjusted as appropriate for condition; otherwise, the actual or latest procurement cost will apply, adjusted as appropriate for condition and market value. An administrative charge will not be applied to rental payments collected under the lease.

2. Since loans to a foreign country are controlled as indicated in MCO 4900.1 and DoD 5105.38-M, the CMC has tasked Code LPO-4 at HQMC with the responsibility of the administration of this program. All requests from a foreign government for a loan of Marine Corps assets must be forwarded to CMC (LPO-4) for action.

3. If the CMC (LPO-4) approves the loan, the MCA will be notified to release the assets.

7001. <u>STATE AND LOCAL LEASES</u>

   <u>NOTE:</u> Specific policy and procedures will be included in this Manual in a forthcoming change.

1. <u>Policy and Background</u>

   a. It is DON policy to cooperate with civilian law enforcement officials of drug law enforcement agencies (DLEAS) to the maximum extent practicable, consistent with the needs of national security and military preparedness, the historic tradition of limiting direct military involvement in civilian law enforcement activities, and the requirement of applicable law.

   b. Assistance may not be provided if the provision of such assistance would adversely affect national security or military preparedness.

   c. All requests from civilian DLEAS for the use of Marine Corps equipment, facilities, or personnel under these orders, including requests which are forwarded with a recommendation that the request be denied, shall be submitted by the regional logistics support office (RLSO) to the CMC (LPO).

   d. The RLSO's are:

      (1) RLSO, Buffalo, New York.

      (2) RLSO, Miami, Florida.

      (3) RLSO, El Paso, Texas.

      (4) RLSO, Long Beach, California.

      (5) RLSO, Honolulu, Hawaii.

2. The CMC (LPO) has been designated as the control point for the Marine Corps for all loan requests from the RLSO's.

3. Public Law 102-190 of 5 December 1991 declared leases (not loans) would be used in support of local and State DLEAS. Further, this change mandated service secretaries charge a "fair market value" for leases in support of local and State DLEAS.

4. The MCA will forward leases to the State or local DLEAS for signature and payment (cashiers check or money order) of a lease

charge for the equipment to be leased. Payment will be made to
the U.S. Treasurer and deposited in MARCORLOGBASES, Albany,
accounts.

5. Once payment is received, the MCA will initiate issue
request to the appropriate inventory manager.

6. The authorized lender will affix signature to the lease,
and a fully executed copy will be forwarded to the lessee.

APPENDIX A

SAMPLE REQUEST FOR RESERVATION OF MARINE CORPS STOCK FOR
GFE/GFM/LOAN

(Revise text, as appropriate; and delete portions not
applicable.)

From: Commander (Code xxx)

To: Commander
       Marine Corps Logistics Bases
       (Code 808-2/MCA)
       Albany, GA 31704-5000

Subj: REQUEST FOR GFE OR GFM OR LOAN RESERVATION

1. Request you reserve the following items for use as GFE or
GFM

or loan for future delivery to. . . . .

for the purpose of. . . . .

   NSN   Nomenclature   Quantity

2. In-the-clear shipping address (DODAAC):

3. Contract number:

4. Valid mailing address (if different from shipping
address):

5. Point of contact and telephone number (DSN and
commercial):

6. Required delivery date:

7. Funding for GFM (SAC 1/2) will be provided by . . . .date
. . . . . :

8. Requester's name and telephone number (DSN or commercial):

9. Any other pertinent information.

APPENDIX B

SAMPLE REQUEST FOR SHIPMENT OF
GFE/GFM/LOAN FROM MARINE CORPS STOCK

(Revise text, as appropriate; and delete portions not applicable).

From: Commander (Code xxx)

To: Commander
       Marine Corps Logistics Bases
       (Code 808-2/MCA)
       Albany, GA 31704-5000

Subj: REQUEST FOR GFE OR GFM OR LOAN SHIPMENT

1. Request shipment of the following items as GFE or GFM or loan

to. . . . .

for the purpose of. . . . .

for CONTRACT NUMBER . . . . . . .previously reserved on

PROJECT CODE. . . . .:

  NSN   Nomenclature   Quantity

2. In-the-clear shipping address (DODAAC):

3. Valid mailing address (if different from shipping address):

4. Point of contact and telephone number (DSN or commercial):

5. Required delivery date:

6. Funding for GFM (SAC 1/2) will be provided by. . . . . .

7. Requester's name and telephone number (both DSN and

commercial):

8. Any other pertinent information.

APPENDIX C

STANDARD MARINE CORPS LOAN AGREEMENT

LOAN AGREEMENT

Project Code X

1. This loan agreement, made in duplicate this _____ day of _____ year _____ by and between the UNITED STATES MARINE CORPS, MARINE CORPS LOGISTICS BASE, ALBANY, GEORGIA 31704, herein called the lender, and _____, herein called the borrower, for the following materiel:

NSN	NOMEN	C/C	U/I	QTY	SUP	EXTENDED SUP	SERIAL NR	DOCUMENT NO.

2. Total Value $

3. Reference:

4. Purpose:

5. Loan Period: From:

6. Obligation Statement of the Borrower:

a. To protect all proprietary, patent, and industrial rights to the property, the information furnished with the property, and the information derived therefrom.

b. To safeguard classified materiel.

c. That accountability and support of materiel on loan are the responsibilities of the borrower.

d. Parties agree that the undersigned individual signs this agreement on behalf of their respective command and, therefore, assumes no personal liability in the event of damage or loss.

e. To assume all responsibility and financial reimbursement for the loss, damage, and the return of materiel without cost to the Marine Corps.

Page 1 of 2

C-1

LOAN AGREEMENT
CONTINUATION SHEET

Project Code X

f. To return all materiel in the same condition code as cited in this agreement and assume all responsibility for any degradation of materiel other than that attributable to normal usage, wear, and tear.

g. Commander, Marine Corps Logistics Bases, Albany, Georgia, reserves the right to determine the final condition code of returned materiel. Financial reimbursement will be provided to the Management Control Activity (Code 808-2), Marine Corps Logistics Base, Albany, Georgia, for materiel requiring repair/replacement by this Command.

h. The lender maintains the right to terminate the loan agreement and recover materiel should operational circumstances so dictate. When requested by the lender, the borrower will immediately return loaned materiel as directed.

i. This equipment belongs to the Commander, Marine Corps Logistics Bases, Albany, Georgia. It cannot be shipped or transferred without authorization from the Management Control Activity (Code 808-2), Marine Corps Logistics Base, Albany, Georgia.

UNITED STATES MARINE CORPS

---------------Seal
M. L. COMBS, Authorized Lender

Date

BARBARA WALTHALL
Point of Contact

DSN 567-6567/68
Telephone

-----------------Seal
Authorized Borrower

Date

Point of Contact

Telephone

Page 2 of 2

C-2

APPENDIX D

INSTRUCTIONS FOR PREPARING AND DISTRIBUTING THE GFM
STATUS REPORT
RCS DD-4400-37

1. Report Heading Columns for Parts I and II

    a. Title. GFM Status Report

    b. Reporting Period. Enter the dates (year and month (YYMM)) that cover the reporting period. 1/

    c. Date. Enter the year, month, and day (YYMMDD) on which the report is prepared. 1/

    d. Report Control Symbol (RCS). Enter the assigned RCS.

    e. DoD Component. Enter the department establishment component code of the reporting DoD component. 1/

    f. Page. Number the pages consecutively.

2. Part I--Shipments of GFM to Contractors

    a. Document Number. Enter the contractor's requisition document number.

    b. Contract Number. Enter the contract number applicable to the contractor's requisition.

    c. National Stock Number. Enter the NSN of the materiel shipped to the contractor (or to a depot pending shipment to the contractor). 1/

    d. Number of Units. Enter the number of units of the materiel shipped.

    e. Quantity Shipped. Enter the quantity shipped to the contractor.

    f. Date Shipped. Enter the year, month, and day (YYMMDD) on which the materiel was shipped to the contractor. 1/

    g. Unit Cost. Enter the unit price of the materiel shipped to the contractor.

    h. Extended Dollar Value. Enter the extended dollar value of the materiel shipped.

    i. Contractor Name. Self-explanatory.

3. <u>Part II--Contractor Requisition Rejected</u>

    a. <u>Document Number</u>. Enter the contractor's requisition document number.

    b. <u>NSN</u>. Enter the NSN reflected in the rejected requisition. 1/

    c. <u>Quantity</u>. Enter the quantity reflected in the rejected requisition.

    d. <u>Reject Status Code</u>. Enter the MILSTRIP status code that indicates the reason for rejecting the requisition as defined in DoD 4000.25-1-M, appendix B16.

    e. <u>Date Rejected</u>. Enter the year, month, and day (YYMMDD) on which the requisition was rejected. 1/

    f. <u>Contractor Name</u>. Self-explanatory

4. <u>Part II (Alt)--Shipment of GFM to Contractor for which Receipt Status is Unknown</u>

    a. <u>Requisition Number</u>. Enter the contractor's requisition document number.

    b. <u>Contract Number</u>. Enter the contract number applicable to the requisition.

    c. <u>NSN</u>. Enter the NSN of the materiel shipped to the contractor (or to a depot pending shipment to the contractor).1/

    d. <u>Number of Units</u>. Enter the number of units of the materiel shipped.

    e. <u>Quantity Shipped</u>. Enter the quantity shipped.

    f. <u>Date Shipped</u>. Enter the year, month, and day (YYMMDD) on which the materiel was shipped. 1/

    g. <u>Unit Cost</u>. Enter the unit price of the materiel shipped.

    h. <u>Extended Dollar Value</u>. Enter the extended dollar value of the materiel shipped.

    i. <u>Contractor Name</u>. Self-explanatory.

    1/ These items have been registered in the DoD Data Element Standardization Program.

5. <u>Distribution</u>. One copy of the report shall be provided to each applicable DoD CAO administering contracts.

APPENDIX E

GOVERNMENT-FURNISHED MATERIEL STATUS REPORT
RCS DD-4400-37

GOVERNMENT-FURNISHED MATERIAL STATUS REPORT
FROM XX/XX/XX TO XX/XX/XX FOR PROJECT:

SHIPMENTS OF GFM TO CONTRACTORS (PART I)

DOC NUM	CONTRACT NUM	NSN	NO. OF UNIT	QTY SHIPPED	DATE	UNIT COST	EXTENDED DOLLAR VALUE	SHIPPED TO

GOVERNMENT-FURNISHED MATERIEL STATUS REPORT
FROM XX/XX/XX TO XX/XX/XX FOR PROJECT:

REQUISITIONS REJECTED (PART II)

DOC	NUMBER	NSN	QTY	REJECTED STATUS CODE	DATE REJECTED	SHIPPED TO

GOVERNMENT-FURNISHED MATERIEL STATUS REPORT
FROM XX/XX/XX TO XX/XX/XX FOR PROJECT:

SHIPMENTS OF GFM TO CONTRACTORS FOR WHICH
RECEIPT STATUS IS UNKNOWN

DOC NUM	CONTRACT NUM	NSN	NO. OF UNIT	QTY SHIPPED	DATE	UNIT COST	EXTENDED DOLLAR VALUE	SHIPPED TO

GOVERNMENT FURNISHED MATERIAL (GFM) STATUS REPORT

1. DATE PREPARED (YYMMDD)	2. REPORTING PERIOD		3. MANAGEMENT CONTROL ACTIVITY (MCA)	REPORT CONTROL SYMBOL
	a FROM (YYQ)	b TO (YYQ)		

PART I - SHIPMENTS OF GFM TO CONTRACTORS

4 CONTRACT NO./ CONTRACT BASIC LINE ITEM NO.	5. CONSIGNEE	6. NSN/PART NO.	7. DOCUMENT NO. (MILSTRIP Requisition No.)	8. UNIT OF ISSUE	9. QUANTITY SHIPPED	10. DATE SHIPPED (YYMMDD)	11. UNIT PRICE	12. EXTENDED $ VALUE

PART II - REQUISITIONS REJECTED

13 CONTRACT NO./ CONTRACT BASIC LINE ITEM NO.	14. CONSIGNEE	15. NSN/PART NO.	16. DOCUMENT NO. (MILSTRIP Requisition No.)	17. UNIT OF ISSUE	18. QUANTITY REJECTED	19. DATE REJECTED (YYMMDD)	20. UNIT PRICE	21. EXTENDED $ VALUE	22. REJECT STATUS CODE (MILSTRIP Status Code)

SAMPLE

DD Form 2543, AUG 89

Page ____ of ____ pages

E-2

INVENTORY CONTROL POINTS GOVERNMENT FURNISHED MATERIAL (GFM) STATUS

REPORTING PERIOD: FROM _____ TO _____

DATE _____

RCS _____

DOD COMPONENT _____

PAGE _____ (Part I)

SHIPMENT OF GFM TO CONTRACTORS

REQUISITION NO.	CONTRACT NO.	NATIONAL STOCK NO.	NO. UNITS	QTY SHPD	DATE SHPD	UNIT COST	EXTENDED DOLLAR VALUE

APPENDIX F

AUTHORIZED VETERANS ORGANIZATIONS

Air Forces Association
Air Reserve Association
American Veterans Committee, USA
American Veterans of World War II (AMVET)
Army and Navy Legion of Valor, USA
Army and Navy Union, USA
Army Mutual Aid Association
Blinded Veterans Association
Catholic War Veterans of the United States of America
Coast Guard League
Disabled American Veterans
Disabled Reserve Association
Irish War Veterans, USA
Jewish War Veterans of the United States
Marine Corps League
Marine Corps Reserve Officers Association
Military Order of the Carabao
Military Order of Foreign Wars
Military Order of the Loyal Legion of the U.S.
Military Order of the Purple Heart
Military Order of the World Wars
National Council of War Veterans
National Eniwetok Veterans Association
National Guard Association
National P-T Veterans Association, Inc.
National Society - Army of the Philippines
National Sojourners
National Tribune
Naval Academy Alumni Association
Naval Order of the United States
Navy Club of the USA
Navy Mutual Aid Association
Regular Veterans Associations
Reserve Officers of the U.S. (ROA, RONS, NROA)
Retired Officers Association
Second Division Association
United Indian War Veterans, USA
United Spanish War Veterans
Veterans of Foreign Wars of the United States

APPENDIX G

ACRONYMS AND ABBREVIATIONS

AAC	Activity Address Code
AECA	Arms Export Control Act
ASA	Appropriated Stores Account
CAC	Cost Analysis Code
CAO	Contract Administration Office
COMMARCORLOGBASES	Commander, Marine Corps Logistics Bases
COMMARCORSYSCOM	Commander, Marine Corps System Command
CMC	Commandant of the Marine Corps
DC	Data Column
DCF	Document Control File
DCMAO	Defense Contract Management Area Office
DFARS	Department of Defense Federal Acquisition Regulation Supplement
DIC	Document Identifier Code
DID	Data Item Description
DLEAS	Drug Law Enforcement Agencies
DoD	Department of Defense
DODAAC	Department of Defense Activity Address Code
DoD SS	Department of Defense Supply System
DON	Department of the Navy
DRPM AAA	Direct Reporting Program Manager Advance Amphibious Assault
FAR	Federal Acquisition Regulation

GFE	Government-Furnished Equipment
GFM	Government-Furnished Materiel
HQMC	Headquarters Marine Corps
LEM	Logistics Element Manager
MCA	Management Control Activity
MCLB	Marine Corps Logistics Base
MCO	Marine Corps Order
MCPR	Marine Corps Purchase Request
MILSTRIP	Military Standard Requisitioning and Issue Procedures
MIPR	Military Interdepartmental Purchase Request
MRC	Materiel Request Confirmation
MRO	Materiel Release Order
MVO	Money Value Only
NavCompt	Navy Comptroller
NSN	National Stock Number
PICA	Primary Inventory Control Activity
PIIN	Procurement Instrument Identification Number
PM	Program Manager
PO	Project Officer or Purchase Order
PRF	Project Requirements File

RCP	Requests for Contractual Procurement
RCS	Report Control Symbol
RDD	Required Delivery Date
RFB	Request for Bid
RFP	Request for Proposal
RIC	Routing Identifier Code
RLSO	Regional Logistics Support Office
RPPOB	Replenishment Parts Purchase or Borrow Program
SAC	Stores Account Code
SECNAVINST	Secretary of the Navy Instruction
SF	Standard Form
SICA	Secondary Inventory Control Activity
U.S.	United States
U.S.C.	United States Code

*U.S. GOVERNMENT PRINTING OFFICE:2000-461-735/20026